HOW APPLYING BEHAVIORAL ECONOMY TO BRING SOCIAL BENEFIT

JOHN LOK

Contents

Preface

Introduction

I write this book aims to let students can have more clear concerns whether how behavioral economy theory can help our society to evaluate why whether the consumer will make the decision, how our societies will be influenced to change, how any why our organizations employees decide to make the performance.

Our sociey is influenced by economic development and consumer behaviors nowadays, why development economy can help our societies to explain why the matter occurs , predict when the matter occurs , even it can help us to solve any social, organizations, consumer challenges.

In my this book, I shall indicate fun questions and the different solution methods in behavioral economy view. Readers can learn more fun behavioral economy suitation in our societies. It divides knowledge and application both parts to let readers have clear understanding whether what behavioral economy means.

Prologue

Table of content

ONE

WHAT BEHAVIORAL ECONOMICS FOCUS ON

(BE) Behavioral economics is primarily concerned with the bounds of rationality of economic agents. Behavioral models typically bring insights from psychology and microeconomic theory. The study of behavioral economics includes how market decisions are made and the mechanisms that drive public choice. Moreover, behavioral economic plays a important role in our lives and in the economy because it can help businesses to explain why we consume the kind of goods and services , the way we do, why we make certain choices of action, the key contibution to behavioral economics, it uses psychological and experimentation to develop theories about human decision making, and has identified a range of biases as a result of the way people think and feel . (BE) is trying to change the way economics think about people's perception of value and expresses preferences.

- Have they relationship between consumer behaviors and economy ?

The success or failure of a nation's economy can greatly affect consumer behavior based on a variety of economic factors. If the economy is strong, consumers have more purchase power and money is spent , f the economy is poor, the reverse is true. Consumer behavior in economics means to explain of how individual cstomers, groups or organizations select, buy, use and dispose ideas, goods and services. A such, consumers play a vitual role in the economic system of a capitalist economy. Without consumer demand, producers would lack one of the key motivations to produce to sell to consumers.

The motivates consumers behavioral economic perspective, it is the new field of behavioral economics has shown them, in practice, people's decisions can be greatly influenced by seemingly irrelevant aspects of their personalities and by the environment in which their decisions are made. So, it seems that consumer buying behavior changes during economic crisis.

In organization how resources choices to use in behavioral economy view, though the number and variety of the different resources businesses require is limitless. Economists divide factors of production into three basic categories:

Land, labour and capital. Land refers to all of the natural resources that businessed need to make and distribut goods and services, labours to make and distribute goods and services, labours refers how the organization chooses to employ the employee skill to make the kind of job, capital refers to how much the organization plans to spend in order to operate its business. Hence, behavioral economy can explains the economic model of employee, human behavior, working performance. It is a representation of people action. The concept is based on traditional economics, where human behavior is believed to spring from absolute rationality.

On behavioral economics in consumer lives and in the economy aspect, it explains it is a game theory, behavioral game theory. It is a game theory , behavioral game theory extened standard analytical game theory by taking into account how players (consumers) feel about the payoffs other players receive, limits in strategic thinking, as well as the effects of learning , the consumer individual past purchase experience, games (choices of purchases) are usually about cooperation or fairness.

For advertising how plays beneficial roles in a healthy economy example, advertising plays a strong role in the economy. It provides useful informatin to consumers that tells them about products and services choices as well as comparing features, benefits and prices, with more complete information, consumers and businesses often choose to purchase additional products and services . Hence, behavioral eonomics draws instead on psychology and economics to explore why people sometimes make irrational decisions, and why and how their behavior does not follow the predictionsof economic models. Because humans are emotional and easily distracted being, they make decisions that are not in their self-interest.

So, behavioral economics is the study of the effects that psychological factors have on the economic decisions making process of individuals. The importance of understanding behavioral economics for marketers is immeasurable as it shows for a better factors that can lead to irrational economic decision, e.g. overspend because of lack of availabiliey, such as buying expense gad because you are in the desert. Another irrational economic decision may be impluse buying or pressure.

- How to apply behavioral economic to explain why the employee does peformance behavior?

A study on human behavior has revealed that 90% of the working population can be classified into four basic personality types: Optimistic, pessimistic, trusting. However, the latter of the four types. Envious is the most common, with 30% compared to 20% of each of the organization whole employee individual economic behavior, economic behavior occurs in a climate of formal and informal organizational rukes. These rules often act as incentives, e.g. appreciation, job promotion, increasing salary. These rules often act as incentives and influence the choices employees make , in general employees chooce to work desk jobs that do not keep to fit, and how they have to make more time to stay healthy.

So, behavioral economic theory explain any organization will need have behavioral skills to dominate employee individual performance to raise. Behavioral skills are interpersonal, self-regulatory, and task-related behaviors that connect to successful performance in education and workplace settings. The behavioral skills are designed to help individuals succeed thorough effecttive interactions, stress management and persistent effort in any organizations.

for task-oriented behavioral skills examples, they may include: active always buy with something, ambitious, strongly wants to succeed, cautious, being very careful, conscientious, taking time to do things right and creative, someone who can make up things easily or think of new things. The six important employee behaviors in organizations are employee productivity, absenteeism, turnover, organizational citizenship behavior, job satisfaction and workplace misbehavior. So, managers need have good behavioral management skills. They are all about learnings appreciation and growth. Take the time to learn, try and grow oen strategies and leadership style.

● How to apply behavioral eocnomic skill to help society to solve challenges ?

The three principles of social economics theory describes how the economy as a whole woks are (1) a country's standard of living depends on its ability to produce goods and services . (2) prices rise when the government prints too much money and (3) society faces a short-run tradeoff between inflation and unemployment. How to use behavioral economics for social impact. According to the American psychological association, social psychology is the study of how individuals affects and are affected by physical environment. Behavioral economics applies these concepts to the economic decisions that people make in addition to the ration thinking. It helps us understand how consumer participate in contest buy products and brand familiar choice in order to make the most rational purchase decison. Also, behavioral economists ask questions mostly about the way people make economic choices, judgements or the way particular financial purchase choice.

Hence, behavioral economic is the study of psychology as it relates to the economic decision making processes of individuals and organizations. In general, our societies ask two important questions: Are economists' assumptions of utility of profit maximization good approximations of real people's behavior? So individuals maximize subjective expected utility?

IN our societies, we need to satisfy and earn the greatest benefit, in economics, rational choice theory, states that when humans are presented with various options under the conditions of scarcity, they would choose the option that maximizes their individual satisfaction. Behavioral economics draws on psychology and economics to explain why people sometimes make irrational decisions and why and how their behavior does not follow the predictions of economic models, e.g. decisions such as how much to pay for a cup of coffee, whether to go to graduate school, whether to pursue a healthy lifestyle , how much to contribute toward retirement.

Because humans are emotional and easily distracted beings, they make decisions that are not in their self interest. For companies are increasingly incorpoarting behavioral economics to incrase sales of their products case example, in 2007, the price of the 8 GB iphone was introduced for $600 and quickly reduced to $400, what if the intrinsic value of the phone was $400? If Apple introduced the iphone for $400, the initial reaction the price in the smartphone market might have been negative as the iphone might be thought to have too pricely. Buy by introdicing the phone at a hgh-pricing and bringing it down to $400, consumers believed they were getting a pretty iphone deal for Apple. So, Apple iphone began to understand tht its phone consumers are irrational, an effective way to behavioral economics in the Apple iphone's decision making policies that concern its internal and external stakeholders may prove to be worthwhile of done properly .

TWO

CONSUMER LEISURE BEHAVIORAL ECONOMY

- Consumer leisure need whether is more and less whether it has what relationship between economy?

Consumer leisure need whether is more and less whether it has what relationship between economy? Also whether the country's economy recession or growth, can it influence consumer leisure need to increase or decrease ? I shall attempt to apply behavioral economy theory to explain whether they have cause and effect relationship as below:

In our societies, there are so many different kinds of leisure activities, also any kinds of leisure consumers can follow the kind of leisure activity's price factor, enjoyable feeling factor, satisfactory feeling factor, lesiure time need factor to influence the leisure consumer individual final choice to which kind of leisure activity among the different kinds of leisure needs. For example, travel leisure activity ought be the most experience, spending of leisure expense to compare general sport lesiure, e.g. swimming , playing basketballs , table tennis, tennis, football, purchae tickets seeing movies, purchase tickets listening music, purchase electronic playing games to stay at homes to play.

In simiarity, it uses only considers leisure price aspect, we shall do the comparable and reasonable decision is that travelling activity ought be the kind of leisure activity, any leisure consumers ought spend the least leisure times to enjoy this kind of leisure activity, e.g. one year has only one time or two-to-five times for overseas for overseas travel. But, in fact, in global there are many travellers, they can make many times of travelling frequent decision, e.g. they can spend one week at least time to go to overseas to travel per month. Hence, it means that global some travellers like to buy air ticket to go to overseas to travel, they spend average one month and one time overseas travel.

In fact, tourism agents hope to attract travellers to choose travelling leisure activity, they will attempt to decrease air ticket price in order to increase travellers number. However, some cheap travelling package price can persuade global some travellers accept to pay cheap price to bu air ticket to spend several days to go to the country to travel enjoy their holidays.

So, it seems that cheap air tcket price strategy, it can attract some countries travellers to accept to spend some time for their overseas holiday their overseas travelling leisure activity can explain why leisure price must be main element factor to influence leisure consumers to reduce spending amount to pay for the kind of leisure activity , such as travelling lesiure activity is one kind of good lesiure activity example.

Otherwise, some kinds of leisure activities, ever their lesiure prices are cheap, it must not influence them to like to spend much time to enjoy them, e.g. swimming, riding bicycles leisure activities, although those kinds of sport leisure activities prices must be very cheap to compare travelling activities , it can must influence many young people like to buy bicycles to ridem even they are proficient bicycle riders or they like to buy tickets to go public swimming pools to swin. The factors may include these both kinds of sports are tired sport leisures, any one must need more body energy to do these sports. Moreover, for student leisure consumers, although these both kinds sports prices, such as bicycles and swimming pool purchase tickets, they are cheap to students, but in fact, students must need to spend time to learn, if they often spend time to enjoy these both of sport activities, they will feel fear that they can not concentrate on spending learning time, if they spend on sport leisure time.

Hence, in behavioral economy view, it explains that lesiure price whether it is high or low, it is not main factor to influence any leisure consumers to do leisure kind of choice, such as sport case to student leisure consumers, they will not choose to spend much time on sport lesiure aspect, because the hard students must feel fear to influence their learning effort when they often spend time on sport leisure aspect. Otherwise, for a sport professonal, e.g. proficient riding bicycle sportman, he may accept to spend expensive price to buy one expensive bicycle , e.g. when he feels the US$3,000 bicycle, it can help him to improve riding speed skills, he won't choose to buy the another US$1,000 bicycle, when he feels that it can not help him to improve riding speed skill, hence, it also explains that the leisure produt high price , it must not influence lesisure consumers number to reduce, it depends on whether the leisure product function to the leisure consumer, e.g. for riding bicycle sport men , they may accept to pay higher price to buy more expensive bicycles , because the hope that the bicyces can help them to comprove their riding speed to more rapid. Otherwise, for student bicycle consumers, they won't compare different kinds of bicycles prices in order to decide whether which kind of bicycles are the most suitable to them to buy to ride.

Hence, behavioral economic theory can explain that price must not be the main factor to influence lesiure consumers' lesiure activities choices, their lesiure need psychological and leisure product individual function factors was also influence their lesiure activities choices.

THREE

Behavioral economy view how DINA biological medical science impact our societies

● Can DNA reproductive technology bring only positive impact to influence our social behavior change?
Human's medical technology had been continue developed to improve to satisfy our medical need, such as cancer patient medical different new drug research, it aims to help future cancer patients to avoid death. However, future human's new medical research will research on DNA biological medical improvement . So, future DNA biological medical technology may bring good or bad social impact, e.g. reproductive animal, such as pig, cow animals . So, when many pigs and cows can be reproduced. Then, pigs and cows number can increase. Consequently, porks beefs meats food number can be also been increased by DNA biological medical reproductive cell technology improvement.

It is good aspect to bring enough meats supply to global , when future DNA biological medical technology can be developed to the reprodctive many cows and pigs number stage in order to raise porks and beefs food number. However, DNA biological cell reproductive technology can also bring bad impact to our society, if one day human can apply DNA biological cell reprodutive technology to reproduce another ourselves, it means that reproductive human why is it bad new? if ne DNA scientist decides to help one country ambitious leader to reproduce himself, then when the country ambitious leader dies, but his another reproductive himself person can aontiue to bring war crisis to global, such as Japan's past leader, he was one ambitious leader to dominate global countries. If DNA reproductive technology is applied to help him to reproduce this Japan ambitious another himself . Then, the another new world

war may be occurred easily. So, I also worry about future DNA reproductive technology may be applied to help the ambitous bad people to reproduce themselves to bring our societies safety and economic recession negative impact. So, it brings this question: Can DNA reproductive technology bring only positive impact to influence our social behavior change? I shall attempt to explain as below:
How does DNA attract our behavior? In some situations, genes play a larger role in determining your behavior. How can genetic technologies impact society ? Although, genetic technology has a great potential to change the medical practice as we know it also has a potential to be misused , it also has a potential to be misused, and lead to further health disparities, discrimination and inequality in the human societies around the world.
However, I believe that those the ways that genetic engineering can help human society. Several works have been done on genetic engineering with major focus on its importance ranging from increasing plant and animal food productio, diagnosing disease condition, medical treatment improvement, as well as production of vaccines and other useful drugs.

- What is the focus of behavioral generics?

Behavioral genetics is the study of genetic and environmental influences on behaviors. By examining genetic influence, more information can be gleaned about how the environment operates to affect behavior. So, in behavioral economic view, gene DNA reproductive cell technology may seem to bring these benefits. Some benefits of genetic engineerinf in agricultures are increased crop yoelds, reduced need for food or drug production, reduced need for pesticides, enhanced nutrient composition and food quality , resistance to past and disease , greater food security, and medical benefits to the world's growing population . Also, the intangible , non economic measurement, possible benefit of genetic engineering may include more nutritious food, tastier food, disease -and-drought resistant plants that require fewer environment resources , such as water and fertilizers, less use of pesticides, increased supply of food with reduced cost and larger shelf life, faster growing plants and animals.
All of these benefits, they can not measured by economic calculation, but they can be felt by us. So, in our social behevioral economic view to genetic engineering, it may bring both positive and negative impact to our societies. On negative impact, these are many risks involves in genetic engineering, the release of genetically altered organisms in the environment can increase human suffering, disease animal welfare, and lead to ecological disasters are positive impact aspect, it can help to defeat diseases, getting rid of all illnesses in young and unborn children potential to live longer, produce new foods, organisms can be tailor-made , faster growth in animals and plants, pests and diseases resistance. But genetic engineering can also bring risks to our societies, e.g. new allergens in the food supply, antibiotic reistance, production of new toxins, concentration of toxic metals, enhancement of the environment for toxic fungi, unknown harms, gene transfer to wild ot weedy relations, change in herbicide use patterns.
By knocking out genes repsonsible for certain conditions, it is possible to create animal model organism of " human disease" as well as producing hotmenes, vaccies and other drugs. So, if DNA can bring human diseases, it means that it can also bring economic loss to our societies, because human disease may bring illness to any one to cause low productivity to any industry development, if the factory has many people human disease from reproductive

animal cell accident risk. Then, the ill worker number increases, low productivities and inefficiencies will cause to the factory. If global has many factory workers got human disease from reproductive animal cell accidently. Then, global factries products producing number must have been influenced to fallen down.

Consequently, global manufacturers will encountered serious loss, due to their products producing speed is slow and their different kinds of products supply number must decrease, if global will workers number increases, they are caused by reproductive animal cell disease. Hence, DNA genetic reproductive technology may also bring global economic loss crisis in possible.

FOUR

EXPLAINING THE RELATIONSHIP BETWEEN INCREASING PROFICIENT WORKERS NUMBER AND AVOIDING EXCESS RESOURCE WASTE

- In organizational behavioral economic view, whether they have cause and effect relationship between employees how to use resources behaviors and organizational resource excess use within organizations ?

In organizational behavioral economic view, whether they have cause and effect relationship between employees how to use resources behaviors and organizational resource excess use within organizations. For example, if the organization has many employees number, whether the organization will use its any internal tangible and intangible resources easily per day.

For construction organization example, one construction organization must need to buy different kinds of construction materials to prepare to let workers to help it to manufacture different kinds of properties or houses (products) in order to sell to property buyers. In its every building construction site, it will need more or less workers, they are needed to use different kinds of construction materials to build housess in different construction sites. I assume that construction site (A), it has 100 construction workers number, every day construction site (A) 100 workers need to use different kinds of construction materials to help them to build 3 building floors wall at least floor number in the construction site (A).

I assume that these 100 construction workers , they include proficient workers and not proficient workers. For proficient construction workers group, they have 50 number, and not proficient construction workers group, they also have 50 number . Hence, the proficient construction workers only need to spend 3 hours maximum and use less number of constructoin materials, then they can finish to build 3 building floors wall per day.

I also assume that all constructoin material supply number is limited. It means that due to this construction firm needs to pre-booking to purchase this kind of the best quality of constructoin material from overseas before three worths. So, it must not have enough time to pre-booking to purchase this kind of best quality of constructoin materials when they are used rapaidly within one month, due to this one month is the final finishing time to this construction firm within one month. Hence, limited construction material supply number and limited finishing time to build this new 40 floors house within this final one month .

So , not proficient construction workers number , limit number of construction material and per day 8 hours which is its limited resources in behavioral eocnomy view. Moreover, total 50 proficient and not proficient 50 construction workers (human resource employees number) will cause this constructoin firm , it will possible need to build this new 40 floors house are more than one month, if these 50 proficient construction workers , they have more than 30 at least number, they are absent to cause their overall construction workers' efficiency to be fallen down, due to the other 50 not proficient constuction numbers must need their teaching how to cooperate ad how use less materials to build this new 40 floor hourse rapidly in order to raise overall constructon team efficiency and avoid to delay more than one month time to build this 40 floors new house successfully within this final one month time.

Hence, it explains that when one organization has more employees, it does not represent that this organization must need to use more resource to achieve its any mission, such as this construction firm case, although it has 50 not proficient construction workers, they need to use more construction materials to build this new 40 floors house in this construction site (A). But, in fact, it has other 50 proficient construction workers, they know how to reduce construction materials to build every building floor wall for this new 40 floors building house. So, they can teach the not proficient building workers to know hoe to avoid to use extra excess constructon material to finish to construct every building fllor wall. SO, although, it has 50 not proficient construction workers number, but they can be taught to learn how to reduce to use these limited the best quality of construction materials to build this 40 floors new house. It implies that if the construction workers number can increase, e.g. increases more 50 not proficient construction workers, this the best quality of construction material resource number must not need to increase demand, because this construction site (A) has 50 proficient construction workers , they can teach these 50 not proficient construction workers how to avoid to use extra excess this kind of high quality construction material to build this new 40 floor house efficiently and effectively within this one month.

Hence, if this construction firm won't have more than 30 proficient workers number is absent in this final one month, it will have enough proficient construction workers to teach these 50 not proficient construction workers to know how to use this high quality of construction materials to build this 40 floors new house building in order to avoid waste or construction material need shortage challenge occurs in this final one month time.

Consequently , it ought finish to build this 40 floors new house building within this month. Hence, it explains why its this kind of high quality of construction material resource need must not increase, because if its all proficient construction workers is absent and their absent number is less than 30, then they have enough proficient construction workers number , they can teach this 50 not proficient construction workers how to avoid to use extra excess construction materials resource number in order to have enough construction material resource supply to satisfy this new 40 floors building house to finish construction within one month finishing date need.

On conclusion, in organizational behavioral economic view, it explains that resource use need must not be influenced to increase when the organization's employees number increase. It depends on whether the organization has how many talent and proficient workers number in order to assist them and teach the not proficient employees how to use resource to manufacture any kinds of products in order to avoid to spend extra excess of resource need. Hence, organizational behavioral economic view, it can explain that any organization's increase to employees number, it does not mean that its resource number is also needed to increase. Moreover, in organizational behavioral economic view, it also explains that if the organization can have many proficient workers to help it to do any complex tasks, they will help it to bring avoiding waste or excess extra resource to use advantage, because they ought know whether how they work, they can help the organization to improve performance or raise efficiency e.g. car manufacture, computer manufacture, television manufcture etc. home electronic products or car leisure products. Due to that manufacturre processes are complex, if the organization can have more proficient high skillful workers to help it to manufacture their products. They ought help it to use lesser manufacturing time and less manufacturing resource to finish any above these products to compare not proficient or low skillful manufacture workers. So, in long time, the organization must may earn economic low cost benefits from proficient worker individual high manufacturing skillful knowledge behavior or performance. So, organizational behavioral economic theory explains why even the organization plans to increase employees number, it's resources number won't be influenced to increase rapidly because when the organization's proficient high skillful workers number is more 2 times at least than not proficient low skillful workers number. They ought have enough effort to train and teach and cooperate with the not proficient low skillful manufacture workers to improve their manufacture skills in order to raise manufacturing efficiency and reduce extra excess resources waste and avoid to bring long term resource waste economic loss. So, any manufacturing organizations must need to increase proficient workers number to assist the not proficient low skillful workers to learn how to improve their skills and know how to reduce to use excess resources to keep to manufacture the highest number of products aim frequently. Consequently, the organization will bring long term low resource use manufacturing economic benefit.

FIVE

STUDENT SUBJECT CHOICE ECONOMIC BEHAVIOR

- What factors influence student makes subject choice decision

Behavioral economic on law and economy subject choice how to student individual subject learning choice behavior in universities economy and law subjects choice example, whether students will make subject either law or economt subject choice, it depends on future lawyer and economist salary whether which occupation can earn long term more salary comparision in order to decide wither law or economy degree learn.

Some university students make these two subjects either one learning choice, they will decide whether school fee is how much more than future salary earns, or personal interest psychological factor influences. So, if the student feels more interest to learn law degree , then he won't choose economy degree between these two degrees. Behavioral economy theory can be applied to explain this student individual economy and law degrees choice behavior because his subject choice decision is depended on personal psychological interest factor more than school fee or future salary possible earn economic salary reward factor influences. But, I assume that if the university can give scholorship for economic and law degree student when the student feels the law degree scholarship higher than economic degree. Then, he will decide to choose law degree to study more than economy degree. He chooses to study law degree because he hopes to earn higher scholarship.

IN behavioral economy principle , it can be applied to explain this student degree choice behavior. However, applying behavioral economy view, it assumes these principles to analyze whether how the student chooses to study the degree. The principles or factors may influence his degree choice may include: Cost and benevits, e.g. the student fee and future salary for the degree, when the student has interest to study law and economic degree. So, he needs to do degree choice. Then, he may compare whether how much law and economy degree school fee, it may be possible future earn salary, scholarship possible reward. All of these factors concern the price for law and economy degree (external cost) and future possible income (salary) for economist and lawyer occupation. It is behavioral law and

economic factor to influence how the student chooses either law or economic degree to study in the university.
For example, when the (A) university on student enrolls to the (A) university before, he needs to choose wither law or economy degree to study. I assume that he only feels interest to study these two degrees. Then, he will compare school fees, if law degree school fee is per year US$5,000, 4 years is US$20,000 and economy degree school fee is per year US$3,000, 4 years is US$12,000. Although, it seems that economy 4 year school fee is more less US$8,000 to compare law degree 4 year, but this student also compare possible future salary for lawyer and economist occupation. He believes that future lawyer salary may pay more 4 times to compare economists salary after 5 years working experience. Although, if this student chooses economy degree to study, he may have chance to earn scholarship if his examination can be good, but it is one time short time economic researd and this scholarship reward is not sure that he must earn, if he can not get at least 5 (A) grade any one economic subject papers in this university economy degree structure. Otherwise, if he chooses to study law and get 5 (A) grade any one law subject papers in the university law degree structure, he can not get scholarship for this law degree. hence , he makes final choice to study law degree, although he can not get scholarship and school fee is more than economy degree. But he believes that he can earn higher salary when he can be one lawyer and he works after 5 years, his salary may be paid more than one economist salary.
In behavioral economic view, it can be applied to explain this university student his degree choice behavior, then he has interest to study law and economy degree. He must need to make one degree choice to graduate, then he may make degree choice decision by external economic cost (degree price) and future reward (possible income) behavioral economic factor . Then, he can judge whether which degree is more suitable to choose to study in this university.

SIX

HOW IMPROVEMENT TO ORGANIZATION BEHAVIOR CAN RAISE ECONOMIC BENEFITS

- How organization improvement may bring economic benefits

Can organizational economies, e.g. transaction cost economics, agency theory, organizational theory , e.g. models of formal organizational independent of the strategies, improve organizational behavior in order to bring economic benefit, e.g. development potentially valuable resources and capabilities, it can raise internal organizatonal strengths and avoid weaknesses in SWOT strategy in order to imporve performance and bring organizational internal economic benefit in organizational behavioral economic view.

For manufacturing industry example, if the car manufacturers can attempt to discover the most efficient steel, or different kinds of car components material, but they can help it to manufacture many high quality cars. Then, their manufactury cost reduce , but its any model of car quality does not caused to poor. Then, this car firm can apply the most efficient and the most high component materials to help it to manufacture high quality cars. Although, it must need to spend time to research how to invest the most efficient and high quality car manufacture components, but if it can apply the most efficient and the high quality components to help it to manufacture any new model of cars. Then, new components research spending time can bring long term low manufacturing cost and high quality of cars to achieve long time economic benefits.

So, on behavioral economic view, organization's spending time on different kind of cheap and high quality car manufacture manufacture components research and research expenditure spending on new kinds of different car manufacture components, it can help it to sell the high quality of different model of cars to satisfy car buyer

comfortable needs. Moreover, it can earn high profit, when it 's any car manufacture component cost reduces. So, SWOT internal strengths (high quality and low cost) to this car manufacturer. It may help it to bring long term raising profit economic benefit, when its any new model of car prices do not need raise, but their compared material manufacture cost reduce, due to new kinds of car manufacture component materials can be invented in success.
Hence, high quality and low cost of car manufacture component invention researching on spending time and research experiment expenditure is value to this car manufacture company, because if high quality and low cost car manufacture component experience succeeds, it can help it to improve any new model of cars quality , but the most important factor is that its any new model of cars prices do not need increase. So, car buyer individual purchase desire won't be influenced to choose any brand of car seller to replace it more easily.
For one drug development process, case example ,I assume that this drug manufacture firm can attempt to spend 10 years time, but it can help it has possible to help it to invent one kind of new pharmaceutical drugs to kill cancer cells for global cancer patients. So, its spending time research on new drugs to kill any kinds of cancers cellers and experimentation expenditure is value, because it can help it to bring economic benefit when global will have many cancer patients believe its new discovery of cancer drugs , it may help them to kill cancer cells to get health or reduce death chance ratio raises after 10 years.
Consequently, in soon future, it's global cancer patients number may increase when they choose to buy its future new cancer drugs paroduct. It may bring high profit economic benefit. So, on organizational behavioral economic view, when the organization spends long time and experimentation expenditure to research new resources, if these new resources can be invented in success and it ensures help it to increase clients number to order to bring future economic benefit. The organization is value to spend time and expenditure to carry on new resources research.

- Can organization apply behavioral economic demand to evaluate work performance for whole different departments?

Behavioral economies investigation may include evaluating demand for a commodity (such as drug experimentation and car manufacturing component material etc.) is given changes in price, using hypothetical purchase tasks, which are a reliable and efficient assessment method. Can behavior management examine work performance evaluation? The work performance evaluation target includes that employee individual and different department will performance evaluation in organization.
I believe high quality or low quality training , which can be evaluated whether the employee individual work performance or the department overall employees work performance can be improved after training. So, if the department employee individual or all employers work performance can be improved, e.g. work efficiency raises, client satisfactory feeling raises, product sale number . Then, the training is a high quality training to help the organization to earn future high economic benefit. Otherwise , if the organization can not earn above any one good result. Then, the training ia a low quality training.So, any organization can attempt to observe any department overall performance and employee individual performance in order to evaluate whether it can provide high or low quality of training to let employees to learn.

So, employee individual behavior can bring performance evidence to let the organization to evaluate whether its training is useful or not useful to achieve its training aim, e.g. when the car manufacturer provides money, time, effort training arrangement to teach all workers to learn how to manufacture car skill. After training provision, many of them, they do not need to work over time more than one hour to manufacture daily of least 10 cars per employee.Before, any one worker must need to spend more than one hour over time to manufacture daily 10 more cars.

So, when this car manufacture skillful improvement train is provided more than one hour more than one hour , none of them, they need work over time in order to manufacture more than at least 10 cars number per day. It seems that training improvement arrangement can be used to evaluate whether employee individual efficiency can be raised in organizational behavioral economic view.

Hence, any organization's internal training provision knowledge resource, it can be evaluated employees' behavioral performance can be improved, about being available to work, about role performance . It assumes that employees are likely to come to work and remain in the organization if they obtain satisfaction from their jobs, and that they are likely to put use effort and work more effectively if they are to be reward more for their effort and performance can be comfirmed to improved by management after they are taught by training. So, when the employee hopes to raise salary, he must hard to learn any new knowledge from the organizational training. Then, training can help the " expectation good reward employees" can improve performance in organizational behavioral economic view.

It is one important successful factor to help the organization to innovate and bring economic benefit, when the organization can implement any new useful training to improve any new useful training to imprve empllyee skills. It means that training is one long term economic organizational strategy, it depends on whether the training is useful or is ot useful in order to help any old employees to raise or improve their skills to achieve raising efficiency and satisfactory client service , sale product number, product manufacture increasing number aims.

SEVEN

CAN ETHICS BEHAVIOR HELP ORGANIZATIONS TO BRING ECONOMIC BENEFIT

- How ethic help organizations to bring economic benefit

Organizational ethic behavior concerns with explaining employee individual behavior in organization, e.g. ethical decision making, ethical conduct for example, when one marketing department manager does not attempt to carrying on any data research about new market research to sell the new model iphone to any country. He only depends on his personal judgement, he believes that this new invention of US iphone producs, they ought to be sell to Korean new iphone market, because he feels Korean must prefer to choose to buy US drand of new iphone products to compare other countries iphone product. However, this iphone marketing development manager lacks enough data research for different Korean iphone buyer age target, purchase experience, purchase desire to conclude Korean iphone buyers must like to buy any brand of US iphone products in preference.

His non ethical new iphone invention decision making to choice Korean ipohone buyers market will bring time waste rick to satisfy Korean iphone buyers' needs to replace other new model ipone users market, e.g. Hong KOng, China, ipone market. So, his ethical decision making to Korean iphone buyers ne iphone invention market may bring less economic benefit to this US iphone manufacture firm. So, this new model ipohone marketing development immoral judgement of this iphone marketing development manager individual decision making to Korean new model ipone invention to Korean ipone users, it can bring high economic loss to this US iphone firm.Otherwise, if this marketing department manager can spend time to carry on data gathering to make more accurate new model iphone invention decision making to choose which one country, then his ethical decision making may help his this US iphone firm to reduce new iphone invention loss risk. So, it explains that why ethic organizational behavior may influence the firm can earn more or less economic benefit. SO, ethic or moral behavior can influence the organization can earn how much economic benefit in long term significantly in organizational behavioral economic view.

- Can improve energy efficiency by organization building occupant's energy consumption relative behavior to bring economic benefit?

Reducing energy consumption in building , it must improve efficiency by building, but whether they have close cause and effect relationship between occupant's energy consumption behavior and improvement energy efficiency to the building? IN fact, high efficiency equipment is being developed, it can help any building to save energy and economic effectiveness, if building energy is subject to uncertainties, such as whether variations, human operations, human behavior changes and government policies. So, building technology equipment improvement may be one main factor to help buildings to save energy . But why occupant behavior may help building to save energy by their daily energy consumption behavior.

The occupant energy behavioral user inputs factor may include: Weather influences, internal heat gain, efficiencies, simplied/ normal occupant behaviors, e.g. a high efficiency chiller can save very limited energy in cold climates due to minimal cooling load, and a good designed natural ventilation building won't work if the occupants do not open windows when outdoor air favors cooling. So, it seems that if one living building hopes to reduce energy consumption, instead of building equipment technological change , e.g. air condition facilities, building occupants , artificial intelligent light, life, their daily energy consumption behaviors, they can influence the living building's energy consumption level in occupant energy consumption behavior and building energy saving economic benefit view.

In fact, when the occupant considers hot water, air condition, energy gas electricity expenditure, he won't use excess electricity, gas resources, because he needs to pay more energy expenditure , when gas and electricity energy consumption expenditure is applied to any business organization offices, warehouses , shops working facilities environment, such as offices, warehouses , shops can often use less electricity, gas energy far ther employees daily work . In long time, the organization must may reduce much electricity, gas energy expenditure for whole organizations business activities. In organizational behavior economic view, organizational energy consumption reduces it can help it to bring less expenditure spending economic benefit.

EIGHT

HOW TO APPLY BEHAVIORAL ECONOMIC THEORY TO EXPLAIN AMAZON BUSINESS E-COMMERCE ORGANIZATIONAL BEHAVIOR

can bring economic benefit to our societies

- Can Amazon e-commerce organization business activities bring ecoonomic benefit to global societies?

Amazon e-commerce is one online product sale e-commerce organization. Any one country e-buyer can use his/her home computer to click to Amazon webstores, when he/she saw the product phone and price, then he/she feels the product's price is reasonable and he/she believes that he/she can make the best choice to buy the product. Then, he/she can pay visa to buy the product from Amazon webstore.

Amazon can bring the most convenient online sale channel to global any one e-buyer. The e-buyer can buy the oveseas product from its e-webstores . He does not need to catch air plane to fly to the e-sellers' shop. he can pay visa to pay the product from Amazon e-webstores any time immediately. All Amazon e-webstores . He can open 24 hours, so all webstores have no close time. So , it can bring busy working people, they do not need to spend long time to visit any shops to make purchase decision. For busy working people example, time has important value to them, they do not want to waste time to make any purchase choice. So, Amazon gives " economic purchase time benefit " to global any one full time working people. In their psychology, Amazon can help them to save much time to go to online shopping purchase chance at homes. They can stay at homes to shopping. Even, when they give their their address to Amazon to know, Amazon will deliver their products to their homes within several days rapidly. Also , they do not need to pay money to buy its products immediately. They can only pay visa to buy the product from Amazon webstores. So, they can save " consumption money" to use for another need in short time. So, one individual e-air ticket buyer, Amazon can bring economic benefit to him, he does not need to buy air ticket to fly to another country to buy the product. Amazon webstores are given more different kinds of similar brand products to let him to choose in order to pay the most reasonable price, working people do not need to spend much visiting shop time to choose any products in order to make the final purchase decision at home rapidly, any one has visa card , he/she can buy the product from Amazon webstores at homes.

Instead of individual e-buyer ecommerce time benefit, spending little time product choice, reducing catching air plane to visit another country seller shop to pay air ticket expense and travelling time spending activities to every e-buyer . Amazon also brings global economic benefits to any one country. When the e-buyer lives in one country to buy the product, it is saved in the overseas country's warehouse. Then, the product must need to deliver to his home by air plane. So, all of Amazon products can bring global goods air transport delivering service to any one overseas buyer, when the product is saved in the overseas seller's warehouse. Any one Amazon product overseas transpor delivery service activity, it can help air goods transport service need increases as well as their goods air transport service income will also increase. Amazon can bring global air goods transport service need increases. It can assist global GDP air goods transport industry grows, and economic benefit for the country's air plan goods delivery service industry development in long term. Hence, on behavioral economic view, Amazon online sale channel ,it can help global economic benefit to air plane goods delviery service industy as well as individual differeent country e-buyer individual time saving and short term money saving economic benefit by visa payment method.

Moreover, Amazon alsoo creates more high technology employment chance to any one country because Amazon owns many offices and warehouses in different countries, due to it is one high technological e-commerce online sale organization, It must need many high skillful website designers to help it to design different countries webstores in order to satisfy any one e-buyer online purchase need. So, it creates high technology job chance to any one country webstore designers . It can help them to raise competitive effort when any one graduate pursues website designer career. IN Amazon provides good employent chance for any one country computer ecommerce designers in order to let them to earn high salary. Also, Amazon public e-commerce organization provides good chance for any one country author to earn royalty income when he/she publishes any electronic or paper books to sell from Amazon publish. It gives good writing skillful authors have more writing chance to help them to sell electronic books and /or paper books from its different countries webbook stores to different countries' readers in short time. It can help them to increase book sale chance to let different countries book buyers can know whether new book topic to the author, he/she will publish soon. So, it brings author's new writing mind training chance when he/she needs to compare book sale rank from Amazon webstores.

Hence, Amazon can bring social employment benefit and author individual skillful training advantage and royalty income benefit to any on country author in nowadays online published industty. So, Amazon online business activities can increase global social employment chance, encourages global authors attempt to train writing skill, helps e-buyers to save visiting shops shopping time and air ticket expenditure for global overseas buyers.

- How and why Amazon e-commerce organization influence global consumee behavioral changes to bring ecommerce benefits to sellers?

In behavioral economic view, Amazon changes consumers behavior as well as product sellers sale method, such as global consumer sellers began to accept online purchase method to replace frequent visiting shop purchase method and global sellers began to accept to apply Amazon webstores to help them to sell products from its online sale channel to replace opening shops locate to the country sale channel.

The advantages to global sellers may include they do not need to pay rent or buy the shops, they can use Amazon webstores to show their different kinds of products photos and prices to let any one online buyer to know . The advantage to global buyers, they do not need to spend time to visit any countries shops to choose products in order to make purchase decision. They only need to spend some time to visit amazon any one country's webstore to see any brands of product photos and know their prices to different kinds of products to compare design and price and functions among of them in the online visiting short time when they stay at home to trun on themselves home computers . So, future home consumption behavior may replace visiting shop consumption behavior. Amazon 's online purchase method will encourage global many sellers have began to believe traditional visiting shop purchase model can not be accepted to global any one consumer more easily, when any one owns computer and internet service at home in common. Then, global shops number will reduce, due to different kinds of product websites purchase model needs number increases to global product sellers, they will close their shops and open themselves webstores or choose Amazon webstore to help them to sell their products conveniently. Consequently, global online purchase and sale transactions number will be influenced to increase by e-commerce organization development.

NINE

WHY CAN GLOBAL CONSUMER BEHAVIORAL CHANGE INFLUENCE GLOBAL ECONOMIC CHANGE

- Have they close relationship between consumer behavioral change and economic change?
- How does consumer behavioral change impact economic change?
- How does cosumer behavior bring positive or negative influence to economic growth or economic recession to the country?

I shall attempt to apply behavioral economic theory to explain their cause and effect relationship why and hoe global economy growth or recession may be impacted by global consumer behavior change reasons ae blow:

I shall indicate travellingleisure and goods air plane transport industries example, since air planes are invented, it is a kind rapid air transport tool, it can help human to do both kinds of transport asrvice, one is goods transport and another is human transport . So, any individual or business goods can be delivered to another country offices or homes by air planes transport tools rapidly. SO, air planes can create more overseas purchase and sale business activities chance between different countries nowadays. Moreover, internet invention, it also increase more e-coomerce online purchase and sale business acitivies to global any one online buyer, he/she only needs to apply computer tool to click to the online seller webstore, when he /she likes the product, he/she can pay visa to buy the product from the onlin seller webstore at home conveniently.

Hence, e-commerce encourages global consumers to choose to buy any products from internet channel, it also brings global goods are needed to transport by air planes between different countries, e.g. one US online buyer makes purchase decision from onlin channel, then he chooses the product from Korean one online seller webstore. After he pays visa to the Korean online seller webstore , then the Korea seller will follow his US address to send the product to the US buyer's home after several days rapidly.

Hence, it explains that if future global consumers like to buy any products from any one country's onine sell webstore. Then, the product must need to be delivered to the online buyer's home. When the seller's product is not located to the online buyer's country warehouse. It needs to be delivered by air plane. When, global there are man consumers, their traditional visiting shops purchase habits are influenced to change online visiting webstores habits. Then, when their purchase habits are influenced to change by rapid, convenient, visa card payment online purchase method at home, time online purchase technological new payment channel method.

In future new online purchase trend development, it may influence future global traditional visiting shops consumption model to change visiting webstores consumption model. Consequently, consumers will choose to pay visa online purchase at home in preference. Also, it encourages visa card purchase , consequently, online purchase may influence these industries development, airlines goods transport service needs increase, it can increase new visa cards number to the frequent online channel e-buyer number. So, online consumption encourages global households save long time money in banks, because we can pay money by visa card payment after we buy any products from online. Global bank may have more money to save longer time from global households, long time money save , because we do not need to withdraw money to buy any expensive products, immediately, e.g. computer , television, furniture etc. When global households begin to accept online purchase method is better to compare visiting shop purchase method. So, future global airline goods transport and bank saving businesses these two industries may have positive impact by future global online buyers raising number.

Hence, when global consumers behaviors began to change online purchase , their online purchase activities may influence global banks can have long time saving money and airlines goods transport need increase rapidly. However, online purcahse activies will bring negative consumers emotion impact to some businesses, e.g. property rent business, because when the country has high population of consumers, they choose online purchases, they won't often vitis shops to choose any kind of products frequently, they only like to stay at home and turn on themselves home computers to find whether global whom sellers, they have webstores to let global consumers to buy their products from online channel. Due to the cuntry willl not have many consumers like to spend time to visit any shops in the country. It means that the country will have many shops are needed to be close, because there are less number peple visit the businessmen shops every day. It will cause property rent service providers can not increase rent income, even decrease rent income, when there are many businessmen close their shops and change onine webstores to replace actual shops. Hence, it seems that online buyers number increases, it may also brings positive impact to influence shop rent service income decreases to the property rent developers.

On global macro economic changing environment, online buyers number increases, it can encourage any kinds of products, they can sell more more easily. So, global product sale number may be influenced to increase rapidly, when global online purchase and sale transactions number increase, GDP on any kinds of product income may be influenced to increase . So, online buyers number increases, it must may bring positive impact to influence global trading GDP high growth, but global shops rent income property developers may be influenced to reduce, due to there are many shops may be caused to close in possible.

How travellers' leisure need change, it may influence travelling leisure service industry development? I shall attempt to explain how COVID 19 disease influences global travellers lesiure need change and airpine and travelling service providers, e.g. hotels, travelling agents, their leisure service needs change. Nowadys, COVID 19 disease has caused global many travellers feel fear to catch airplanes, because air planes all windows are needed to close, he/she has COVID disease, then he/she can bring any one passegner to get this kind of disease by air plane close window air environment. So, when globa many travellers feel afreaid to catch air planes, this kind of COVID 9 air contact disease, it can cause global travellers number has began to reduce, many of travelles began to reduce travelling times per year, even 0 time travel per year. Consequently, it will bring negative impact to global travelling industry development.

Firstly, COVID 19 disease influences global traveller individual travelling desire decreases, every traveller began to avoid to catch air planes to travel. So, any country;s airlines air planes flying times began to reduce, because it is no full seats booking to any airlinees. It means that airlinee must decrease income, alsoo they need to pay parking airplanes rent to any countries airports. So, fixed rent expenditure will need to pay, and many airlines began to dismiss the excess extra number of airline front service staffs, e.g. airport front service staffs, air plane check in /out staffs, even pilots number began also decreased.

So, airline unemployment ratio increases , it causes pilots, airlines service staffs need to change jobsm even some coutnries pilots , choose to do simple goods delivery jobs in supermarkets or securities. Also, COVID 19 disease influences hotels, travelling agents income began to reduce, because there are none many travellers need to live hotels, and they do not need travelling agents to help them to arrange any travelling journeys. So , COVID 19 disease influences many different countries travellers began choose any leisure activities to replace travel, because they feel afraid to get COVID 19 disease when they need to sit in closed window air plane environment.

This kind of disease can influence any one travller individual leisure choice began to change, such as they began to forgive travel siure activities, they will spend holiday to do other leisure activities in themselves countries , e.g. climbing mountain, swimming, running, playing table tennis, tennis etc. different outdoor sports. all of these leisure sports have same features, global any one leisure needer, he does not catch air plane to fo to another country to carry on playing these any one sport and he/she does not need to pay more price to enjoy these sports. Otherwise m travelling leisure activity, it must need any one leisure needer to spend much expenditure to enjoy this kind of leisure activity . So, it explains why many travellers beagan to choose to do any kinds of sports to replace spending money to enjoy travel leisure in their holidays,

On conclusion,m this COVID 19 disease had influenced global travel leisure businesses and travel related leisure service industries income and travellers number began to reduce and any countries GDP on travelling industry will have negative economic recession occurrence in this COVID 19 disease global envionment. Hence, it implies thaat consumers (travellers) behavior leisure activities need, it may influence global business activities increase or decrease , global economic growth or recession, they have close cause and effect relationship between consumer behavioral change and industries GDP changes in behavioral economic view.

TEN

CAN ECONOMY EFFECTS STUDENTS' ACADEMIC PERFORMANCE

● Can student individual financial situation or economic environment influence individual learning performance ?

Why does student enrollment rise when the economy recession? When a strugging economy certainly forces extra pressure on young students seeking funds for loans and tuition cost, the enrollment rates for colleges continuous to rise. In fact, some experts theoritize that a poor economy environment actually helps a stimulate student enrollment. Whether it is the economy , new academic programs or better recruiting, community colleges are seeing an enrollment boom, when enrollment has been growing steadily , it may increase year institutions. To help prospective student interests when providing all current students with diverse support.

What the motivation had factors that are encouraging students to enroll, e.g. whether it is that the country 's young people feel the country begins have poor economy, so many of them choose to enroll schools to learn new knowledge, because scoial poor economy environment, it won't have many employers like to pay more salaries to employ new employees, consequencey, unemployment rate will rise, it causes students feel difficult to find jobs to do in general, even graduate students. So, it seems that economy recession may encourage students further study, because job supply is decreasing. so, it causes many young people choose to spend time to further study in order to wait economy recovery later. Then, they can prepare to seek any new jobs more easily when there are many employers like to increase employees number.

So, it explains that they have case and effect relationship between student enrollment number and the country's economy growth or recession or recovery, For example, when the country economy growth, in society, it will have many employers like to spend more salaries to employ new employees, because there are many people like to consume, when most of them have jobs to do and earn higher income. so, it seems that in society consumer individual increasing consumption attitude/desire that can help businesses grow, when businesses have more customers, they have effort to pay money to buy any things to use.

Businessmen ought need to increase employees number to help them to develop themselve businesses more successfully. So, it is economy growth period, moreover, many young people feel economy growth can create more employment chance in society. So, it encourages many students choose to forget to continue to pursue high level academic education, e.g. when the student had graduated undergraduate degree, due to he feels social economic environment is improved. So, employers are seeking new employees to help them to develop businesses. So, employment chance increases and salaries level will also rise. So, it encourages many undergraduate students do not want to pursue master degree. Because they believe that they can find jobs to do more easily in this time. So, it seems that the society's present economy suitation is either goos or worse, it can impact students to choose continue pursue higher learning stage or not. So, it explains that student individual learning desire and the social economy have close influential relationship.

● Why does economy scenarios can influence student learning behavior?

Why does economy scenarios can influence motivation and learning behavior on student achievement? Quality in higher education is not only determined by lecturers, it also depends on student individual learning desire, because if economy scenarios can influence the student learning desire to pursue continue learning or seek jobs in society. Then, quality in higher education won't be main factor to influence student individual learning in success or failure. If the student does not plan to continue to learn, even the school has good quality in higher education , it won't attract the student to choose to enrol to the school to continue learn easily. It is due to whether economy scenarios how influences the student decides to pursue or forget further study.

In fact, any countries must encounter or experience economic recession or economic growth or economic recovery period different social economic environment changes. It will bring negative or positive emotion impact to the country's every student learning attitude, in order to decide whether continue pursue learning is better or forget pursue learning is better. So, school fee whether is high or less, it is not main factor to influence student individual continue learn.

In macro economic view, the social's economic growth, or economic recession or economic recovery , any one of these economic scenarios change, it will bring positive or negative emotion impact to encourage the student either chooses to further learning pursue or forgive further learning pursue, in student further learning social behavioral economic view.

ON conlusion, on behavioral economic analytical theory, it explains our social macro economic environment new changes to be better or worse, it may bring indirect impact to influence the country's student individual learning desire or learning behavior either on pursue continue learning or forget continue learning in global societies. So, it also implies that whether the school's fee whether it is more or less, it is not main factor to influence student individual continue pursue to learn or not. If the student feels that movement, himself/herself country's social economic scenario is worse, or it is experiencing recession. The student will be influenced to choose continue to go to school to pursue further learning. So, worse economic environment or recession macro economic environment feeling, it may persuade any country's students trend to choose to pursue further study intention more than seeking jobs to work intention, because they feel social jobs provisin chances are influenced to reduce, and no many jobs to supply to them to choose, salaries will be reduced etc . these factors , they can caes the country will have many students make school enrollment choice more than seeking jobs choice. Hence, I believe that any country students school enrollment choices, they have close relationship to themselves country's economic scenario changes at the moment. Hence in behavioral economic view, it may explain why and how any country's economic environment can bring either positive or negative emotion influence to persuade or dissuade the student chooses to either continue further academic study or forgive continue further academic study. So, behavioral economy theory is one kind of new economy and psychological science. Psychologists can apply this theory to research and explain and conclude how and why our social economy change can impact students, consumers, households, businessmen believe in order to make rational decision to earn more economic benefit and avoid economic loss. Also, behavioral economy theory also may help psychologists and economists to predict how and why our societies will ought to be changed to be better ot worse by which kind of factors accurately. So, it may help government leaders or businesses organizations decision makers to do more accurate decisions or strategies to solve any challenges in success.

ELEVEN

CAN DRIVING TIME REFLECT INCOME LEVEL

● Can behavioral psychologist apply vehicle owner individual driving times to measure or evaluate whether he/she has high income level or whether his/her income increases or decreases?

Can drivers' driving time reflect his/her general income level ? In general, whether private car owners , their driving times can be influenced by income changing level? It depends on different factors, e.g. the car driver does not want often spend 10 minutes to wait bus from home to working places or from working places to home two ways frequently.

I assume that, in general, private car owners do not want often drive themselves cars to go to anywhere, e.g. working people usually only like to drive themselves cars , when they need to work, even holiday leisure activity, they need to drive cars to arrive the leisure activity destination. So, it seems that any car owners , their cars purchase aims, they are either for working needs or leisure aims mainly. So, I bring this question: Suggesting that any countreis car owners, their cars purchase usually for leisure and working both intention. Can the car owner's per month driving times, it can reflect his/her income level whether it increases or decreases? It means that the car owner will increase driving car times, when his salary has increased or the car owner will decrease driving car times, when his salary has decreased? Can driving car times represent the car owner his/her general increasing or decreasing salary? Have they relationship between increasing or decreasing to car owner's driving times and his/her salary increasing or decreasing level?

Behhavioral economists can attempt to apply behavioral economic view to research general car owners their driving behaviors. In general, when can fuel price increases, it may influence car owners to reduce driving times because when they drive themselves cars frequently, their cars must need to use much fuel. Consequently, they will need to pay higher price to buuy another long driving time useful fuel. So, when any one car owner knows that car fuel prices are general increasing. They will be influenced to reduce to drive themselves cars to avoid more expenditure spending

on car fuel aspect.
So, I assume car fuel price increases, it can influence general car users reduce themselves driving car times per day. They won't drive themselves to go to far destination, uness the destination is not too far. It means that general car owners like to drive cars to go to short distance destination only, if general car fuel price has increased significantly in local car fuel market. Hence, it seems that car fuel price whether rises up or falls down, it can influence many car owners avoid often drive themselves cars to go to long distance destination, in order to avoid frequent high fuel price expense. Also , it means that any car fuel seller ought not often rise fuel price in order to avoid many car owners reduce driving times behaviors. Consequently, car fuel and car purchase number will be influenced to reduce when the country has many car owners reduce driving times to go to long distance destination. It is driving car and using car fuel behavioral market principle, it means that when the car fuel price general increases, it influences general car owners reduce driving car want more times, because they do not want often buy new car fuel ar rising price level to avoid not essential economic loss on rising price of car fuel expenditure.
Hence, if this supposion to " general rising car fuel price level, " it will influence general car owners avoid to drive themselves cars to go to long distance destinations. It is reasonable and their driving car times will be influenced to reduce in society. Then, it explains that behavioral economists can attempt to gather general social car owner individual driving car times increases or decreases between last month and this month to evaluate whether it is direct car fuel price as well as whether it rises or falls down. This factor can judge whether what factor can cuse general car owner individual driving times increases or decreases in society. Also, it implies that we can depend on general car owner individual driving behavioral times to judge whether the car owner's salaary level had been increased or had been decreasing in the past. It is possibe that general social car owner individual driving time behavior is significantly increasing or decreasing, it may reflect whether the car owner has present salary , it has been increasing or has been decreasing. Because if the car owner whose salary has been decreasing significantly, the significant decresaing salary, it may influence the car owner reduces to spend long time to drive car to arrive another long distance far away destination frequently. The reason is that he avoids to increase economic loss to use more car fuel for non essential driving use, when he feels that his income is significantly decreased.
Hence, any behavioral economists may attempt to gather household individual general expenditure data in order to conclude what factors influence the household changes his/her family behavioral consumption or consumption attitude. It means thay any household individual consumption attitude changes, it may be influenced by any product price changing factor, such as car fuel price case or the household overall rising or falling income level factor in household behavioral economic view.

Printed by Libri Plureos GmbH in Hamburg,
Germany

9 798886 842227